FOR GROWING CHRISTIANS

DISCIPLESHIP

BY SELWYN HUGHES

QUIET TIME

Dear Heavenly Father,
I know you never have liked
all my good motives
with no action,
nor enthusiastic action
without proper motives.
Sometimes I despair of ever
getting the two together
often enough
to really please you.
And, as I simmer about it
it boils down, again,
to the same thing:
YOU provide everything in
me
that pleases you!
Your word says,
"For God is at work within
you
helping you WANT to obey
him,
and then helping you DO
what he wants."
Tomorrow, Lord,
will I learn to stop trying
and start trusting?

Susan Lenzkes
© by author

WHAT IS A DISCIPLE?

For Reading and Meditation: Matthew 10:1–11

"He called his twelve disciples to him and gave them authority to drive out evil spirits ..." (v. 1)

Throughout the Gospels one term is used more than any other to mark the relationship between Christ and His followers – and that word is *disciple*. Jesus used it frequently to identify those who were close to Him and, following His return to heaven, the word passed into the Acts of the Apostles, where it is used in the same way.

Some are surprised that the word does not occur in the Epistles (the letters written to the different churches), and one possible explanation is that the Epistles were mostly addressed to Christians as members of local churches, and not as individuals. The word "disciple" simply means "a learner", or "a trained one", and is used to identify the original group of twelve disciples who accompanied Christ on His travels, as well as other followers of Christ who were not part of the original twelve. The word appears about 260 times in the Gospels and the Acts. Disciples are those who gather around a teacher, and are trained by him, until they evaluate his words, learn his secrets, and copy his lifestyle.

IS DISCIPLESHIP OUT OF DATE?

Some feel that the teaching of *discipleship,* as outlined in the New Testament, is completely out of place in this modern world. "It was easy," they claim, "in the days of Jesus when the world moved at a different pace, but now ...?" To surrender to this mood is to live on a lower level than God intended, for the truths underlying discipleship are not only capable of fulfilment, but are, in fact, the only way in which God can be glorified by His people. *Discipleship is God's standard for all believers, in all denominations, at all times, in all places of the world.*

> *The word "disciple" simply means "a learner", or "a trained one".*

Lord, help me not to live on a lower level when Your Spirit beckons me toward the life of full discipleship. Enable me to be a fully committed disciple every day of my life. Amen.

TRUE CHRISTIANITY
For Reading and Meditation: Acts 11:19–26

*"... The disciples were called Christians first
at Antioch." (v. 26)*

We ended yesterday by saying that discipleship is God's
standard for all believers, at all times, in all places of
the world.

In the Book of Acts, "disciple" is the term used most
often to refer to believers. In fact, Christ's followers were
called disciples *before* they were called Christians. Luke, the
writer of Acts, uses the word "saint" only four times, and
the word "Christian" but twice. The word "disciple", however, is used twenty-two times. A fair conclusion unfolds,
namely, that *every Christian is a disciple.*

PSEUDO-CHRISTIANS

In some circles the word "disciple" has come to mean
something set apart from normal Christianity, as if disciples
were a special breed of their own. A well-known phrase
passed around in evangelical circles has helped to reinforce
this idea: "You can be a Christian without being a disciple,
but you can't be a disciple without being a Christian." I
seriously question the truth of these words, for if my
understanding of the New Testament is correct, then the
principles of discipleship as outlined by Jesus Christ are
intended to be an integral part of our Christian commitment. Unless they are present in our everyday experience,
we are no more than *pseudo-Christians.*

"True Christianity," said Evan Hopkins, "is an all-out
commitment to the Lord Jesus Christ. The Saviour is not
looking for men and women who will give their spare
evenings to Him – or even weekends – rather He seeks
those who will give Him *first* place in their lives." He looks
today, as He has ever looked, not for crowds drifting aim-
lessly in His track, but for those who are prepared to follow
the path which He Himself trod.

*Every
Christian
is a
disciple.*

**O Jesus, Lord and Master, Your words "Apart from me you can
do nothing" come home to me today with renewed emphasis. I
can only be Your disciple as I let Your life flow into me. So help
me, I pray. Amen.**

THE GOAL

For Reading and Meditation: Matthew 10:16–24

" 'A disciple is not above his teacher, nor a servant above his master.' " (v. 24, RSV)

We must spend another day in making sure that we properly understand the meaning of the word "disciple".

We said the other day that a "disciple" is "a learner" or "a trained one". Christ's disciples are those who draw near to Him to seek after truth and, sitting at His feet, learn from the unfolding of His lessons, the ways and will of God for them. In obeying each successive word they discover that His personal presence transmits an uplifting power which enables them to live up to the demands He makes. Not only does He lift the standards to almost unbelievable heights, but He also provides the power by which we attain to them. There are, of course, as we shall see, stern requirements guarding the entrance to the life of discipleship, but our first concern must be to discover the relationship which Christ has, as Teacher, to those who are called His disciples. The Master is not just a lecturer with a vast knowledge of a certain subject, from whose messages we make applications to ourselves; nor is He merely a prophet – making pronouncements and leaving the issues for God to work out.

MASTER-TEACHER

The goal is to be like Jesus.

He is the *Master-Teacher* who possesses full knowledge, and bends over every pupil with a set purpose in view, imparting such knowledge as the disciple needs to cover every step, and moving always toward a predetermined end. And what is that predetermined end? In a phrase – *to be like Jesus*. "From the very beginning God decided ... that we should become like His Son" (Romans 8:29, TLB).

Father, something is burning in my heart as I contemplate my eternal destiny. You have made me for Yourself and my heart will never be fully satisfied until I am transformed into Your likeness. Amen.

WHO AM I?

For Reading and Meditation: Matthew 10:37–39

" 'Whoever finds his life will lose it, and whoever loses his life for my sake will find it.' " (v. 39)

We are beginning to see that every Christian has the potential to be a first-class disciple. This is because of the personal interest which our Master takes in each one of His students.

Before I became a Christian I was repelled by the thought of enrolling in Christ's school of discipleship, as I felt to do so would be to give up all rights to my individuality. I looked upon discipleship as being confined to a classroom from which there was no escape, and being forced to listen to boring sermons which had no relationship to modern-day living. The idea of being part of a life experience in which *so many were involved* horrified me, as I felt it left no room for the development of one's individuality. I viewed Christ's disciples as being faceless people who wore the same uniform, said the same things, and moved like robots through society.

THE CRISIS WAS OVER

How wrong I was! When I finally surrendered to Christ, I did not lose my individuality – *I found it.* I saw that, prior to conversion, my identity was vague and nebulous, for I had never discovered *who I really was*, but when I surrendered to Christ, and became one of His disciples, the identity crisis was over. When the question thrust itself upon me, "Who am I?" the answer came – "I am Christ's disciple."

In case anyone thinks, as I did, that discipleship means a loss of personality, then just throw yourself down at Christ's feet, surrender your whole being to Him, and you will, for the first time in your life, *discover who you really are.*

I did not lose my individuality – I found it.

O Father, how true it is that I cannot discover my true identity until I lose myself in You. I am beginning to see that when I am in You, and You are in me, then, and only then, am I aware of who I really am. Amen.

A PERSONAL RELATIONSHIP
For Reading and Meditation: Mark 2:14–17

"As he walked along, he saw Levi ... 'Follow me,' Jesus told him ..." (v. 14)

Slowly the thought is shaping itself in our minds that to be a disciple of Jesus Christ is the highest calling, and the grandest destiny of every human being. If one can answer the question, "Who am I?" by saying, "I am Christ's disciple," he is on his way to complete fulfilment as a person.

GOD IS PRESENT EVERYWHERE

We said yesterday that Christ takes a personal interest in each one of His children, and therefore discipleship must not be seen as sitting in a class listening to lectures, but receiving the *individual attention* of the Master in every circumstance and situation. It is a *discipling process* in which He bends over us, intent on getting us to properly absorb one principle before moving on to another. It may be difficult for us to understand how He can give each one of us His *personal* attention when there are so many others to teach and train, but then, remember that our Master is none other than the Living God who is *everywhere present.*

Our relationship with Christ, as His disciples, is on a personal level from the moment we are converted to the moment we graduate in His eternal presence. If a person is not *personally* converted then he is not converted in the Biblical sense, and if he is not personally discipled by Christ, then he can never be a disciple in the Biblical sense. Discipleship is not the embracing of an idea, *but commitment to the Person of Christ.* It is not Christ's teaching which makes us disciples, but His personal presence in that teaching. In discipling us, He gives Himself to us as if there was no other human being in the universe.

Disciple-ship is commitment to the Person of Christ.

O Father, I am so thankful that in drawing me to Yourself, You have not tied me to a principle but linked me to a Person. I am Yours, and You are mine. Thank You, dear Father. Amen.

EVERY DISCIPLE IS UNIQUE

For Reading and Meditation: Psalm 139:1–18

*"You were there while I was being formed in utter seclusion.
You ... scheduled each day of my life before I began to
breathe ..." (vv. 15–16, TLB)*

We are attempting to overcome the charge made by many that Christian discipleship is responsible for turning people into dull conformists to a lifeless tradition.

HEIGHTENED UNIQUENESS

Religion may produce a dull sameness in people, but Christianity does not. Sameness and conformity are non-Christian attitudes, for the Bible teaches that there is a uniqueness about every single human being ever made, and in conversion that uniqueness is not lost, but heightened. God created our human personalities with an even greater variety than the autumn leaves, snowflakes or sunsets. God does not intend us to become carbon copies of each other, for even those who are just one-talent people have possibilities that cannot be duplicated by five-talent people. God has a custom-tailored plan for each individual life, and He is working with each one of us personally, to perfect this plan and bring it to completion.

In the discipling process God never loses sight of a person's uniqueness, and the Church would do well to recognise this, for spiritual effectiveness will increase and abound when every Christian is taught to be his individual self, and express his uniqueness, in creative ways.

When God made this earth He made it out of something which was "without form and void", *and He calls His disciples to the same kind of activity in the world today.* He wants you to use your uniqueness and creativity to turn an enemy into a friend, an adversity into an adventure, and evil into good.

God has a custom-tailored plan for each individual life.

O Lord, every part of my being cries out with joy at the discovery that my Creator has designed me to be a creative person. Help me to discover my uniqueness, and to use it this day – and every day – to the glory of Your Name. Amen.

CREATED – TO BE CREATIVE

For Reading and Meditation: Ephesians 2:4–10

"For we are His workmanship,
created in Christ Jesus to be creative."
(v. 10, literal translation)

We must spend another day exploring this thought of a Christian's uniqueness, for unless we see this truth and apply it daily in our lives we will never move on to be effective disciples.

We said yesterday that creation was making something good out of something that was not good – "the earth was formless and empty, darkness was over the surface of the deep" (Genesis 1:2). This is the challenge which God brings to each one of His disciples – to bring order out of disorder, cosmos out of chaos, and life out of death.

A CREATIVE LIFE

Creativity is not restricted to such things as composing symphonies, writing sonnets and painting portraits. Only a few people have talents for composing, writing and painting, but God desires that *everyone* should become a creative person, expressing his own uniqueness in such daily activities as bringing up a family, teaching a class, working in a factory, running a business, typing in an office, or driving a truck. Each one of us has received from God the necessary gifts to live a creative life, and the sooner we see this the more effective our lives will become.

When a housewife meets the chaos of a busy household and brings order to it, she is creative. When a teacher faces an apathetic class, and makes learning an adventure, she is creative. When a business man sincerely and honestly serves the best interests, not of himself, but of others, he is creative. When a factory or office worker meets an impossible situation with courage and integrity, he is creative. When the Creator of the universe inhabits our beings, then He enables us to be creative too.

> *God desires that* **everyone** *should become a creative person.*

O God, I am beginning to see that when You created me, You planned for me to be creative too. Help me to follow my Master's designs for me in everything I touch this day. In Christ's Name. Amen.

WE NEED A NEW CALIBRE
For Reading and Meditation: Acts 4:31–37

*"All the believers were one in
heart and mind ..." (v. 32)*

It is now time to ask ourselves a pointed question: "Why is it that with such clear teaching as the New Testament gives on the subject of discipleship, we are not seeing more men and women of the calibre of the early disciples?"

It could be that many of our churches are not geared to the production of such disciples. There are signs, of course, that things are changing, but for far too long Christians have thought that all there is to being one of Christ's disciples is to attend church on a Sunday, listen to a sermon, sing a few songs – and that's it. The blame for such a negative idea of discipleship must lie largely with those Christian leaders who have not seriously got down to the business of training their people to become disciples in the real sense of the word. One of the greatest gaps that exists in the present Church is between *belief* and *behaviour.* We have been guilty of telling people *what* to do, without telling them *how* to do it. We have given *exhortation* without *explanation,* and have stressed the *what* without explaining the *how.*

PROGRAMME FOR PRODUCING DISCIPLES

The result is that there are thousands of Christians in our churches every Sunday who sit listening to marvellous sermons and say in their hearts, "This is a fascinating sermon, but why doesn't someone help me with my problem?" The production of disciples, in the New Testament sense, should be the major activity of every church that names itself with the Name of Christ. Every church should have its own programme for producing disciples. If it hasn't, then something is seriously wrong.

One of the greatest gaps that exists in the present Church is between **belief** *and* **behaviour.**

O Father, with the world facing the greatest problems of human history, stir up Your people to face the challenge of producing disciples of the calibre we read about in the early Church. In Christ's Name. Amen.

HOW ARE DISCIPLES PRODUCED?

For Reading and Meditation: Ephesians 4:4–13

"Why is it that he gives us these special abilities ...? It is that God's people will be equipped to do better work for him, building up the church, the body of Christ ..." (v. 12, TLB)

We said yesterday that every church should have its own training programme for producing modern-day disciples.

When I first wrote that statement I wondered if it might offend, but then I realised that if it is true, and conveyed in a spirit of love, then it would not hurt or hinder, but help. Let's face the fact together that one of the missing ingredients in today's Church is the *how-to-do-it*. People need help in overcoming the basic problems which they face day after day, and until we close the gap that exists between *belief* and *behaviour,* we will not see the kind of disciples which the New Testament so clearly portrays.

TRAINING PROGRAMMES

When our churches move toward having their own training programmes, then para-church organisations like Youth With A Mission, Campus Crusade for Christ, The Navigators, CWR and others can be phased out, or work more in line with local church needs. If every local church had a plan and programme for the spiritual development of its people, in line with the New Testament teaching on discipleship, then many servicing organisations would have no further reason for their existence. We have a long way to go before this happens, of course, but in the interests of the unity of the Body of Christ it must be one of our future goals.

TEACHING AND TRAINING OTHERS

How can churches go about the task of making disciples? By each minister investing his time and talents in a small group of people and equipping them with his own insights, training and experience so that they, in turn, can teach and train others. This is God's way – and the only way – by which disciples can be made.

People need help in overcoming the basic problems which they face day after day.

O God, lay Your hand upon every minister called by You to this privileged position, and use them to build an army of true disciples who will show to the world a new approach to life. In Christ's Name. Amen.

THE FIRST STEP
For Reading and Meditation: Acts 2:22–39

"Peter replied, 'Repent and be baptised, every one of you, in the name of Jesus Christ for the forgiveness of your sins ...' " (v. 38)

We continue looking together at some of the reasons why our churches are not producing disciples of the calibre found in the early Church.

We saw that one reason for this could be the fact that many churches do not have a serious plan or programme for making such disciples, but perhaps a more basic reason is that many churches lack in their preaching and teaching *a firm emphasis on the need for true repentance*. The first step into discipleship is through repentance, and it is the primary plank in the Christian foundation. Discipleship begins with a decision – a decision to repent – which involves turning from one's self-centredness, to confess that *Jesus is truly Lord*.

SUPERFICIAL PREACHING
Much of today's evangelical preaching is superficial, in which people are invited to come to Christ on their terms – not His. Someone, describing the modern-day approach to evangelism, said, "The person being witnessed to is presented with a series of quick-fire questions, such as 'Do you believe Christ is the Son of God?' 'Do you believe He died for you?' 'Do you now admit He is the Saviour of the world?' If the answer to these questions is 'Yes', then a decision card is put under the person's nose with the added remark – 'Sign here'."

If we bring people into the Christian life without making clear the need for true repentance, then their subsequent experiences will be fraught with a great deal of insecurity. Vance Havner, a well-known Christian author, says, "Today cheap grace is being preached, and received by cheap faith, resulting in cheap Christians."

"Cheap grace is being preached, and received by cheap faith, resulting in cheap Christians."

Heavenly Father, keep my heart ever open to the fact that I can never know the reality of Your saving power until first I have demonstrated my willingness to repent. Help me, and help others to understand this. In Christ's Name. Amen.

THE PRIORITY OF REPENTANCE

For Reading and Meditation: Luke 5:29–32

" 'I have not come to call the righteous, but sinners to repentance.' " (v. 32)

We saw yesterday that repentance is the primary plank in every Christian's foundation, and without this there can be no continuance in the Christian life.

Repentance means a change of mind, in which a sinner changes his mind from what he believes to what he knows God believes. As the root of sin is self-centredness, it is from this we must turn if we are to experience the salvation of God in the way the New Testament unfolds it.

THE ONLY WAY IN

Charles Finney, the great revivalist of a previous generation, saw and witnessed the genuine conversion of thousands of souls because of his insistence on the need for a real and radical repentance. He presented the claims of Jesus Christ in such a way that people *had* to repent in order to become Christians. His was no "slip-into-the-kingdom-by-the-side-door" type of evangelism, but a confrontation with sinners that led them to see the only way into the kingdom of God was through the door of a real repentance.

The word "repentance" implies the conviction that God is wholly right and the sinner is wholly wrong. When a person comes into the Christian life with this conviction clearly established, he has discovered a significant principle which enables him, in each subsequent encounter with God, to agree with the Almighty and believe that *He* is always wholly right and never wrong. We do not do people true service unless we confront them with the important issue of repentance, for without it there can be no meaningful continuance in the Christian life.

> *God is wholly right and the sinner is wholly wrong.*

Lord, I come to You today believing that You are wholly right and I am wholly wrong. I cannot trust myself, but I know I can trust You. Thank You, Father, for helping me to see this today. Amen.

WHAT REPENTANCE IS NOT

For Reading and Meditation: Matthew 3:1–12

"In those days John the Baptist came ... saying,
'Repent, for the kingdom of heaven is near.' " (vv. 1–2)

We are seeing that without true repentance, no one can become a disciple of the Lord Jesus Christ. They may take on themselves the *name* of a Christian and hide behind the screen of a religious faith, but unless there is real repentance there can be no real conversion.

THE IMPORTANCE OF REPENTANCE

The importance of repentance is quite clear when we examine the Scriptures. God commands it (Acts 17:30). It was the reason for Christ's coming into the world (Luke 5:32). It was part of the commission given to the early disciples (Luke 24:47). It is necessary for an entrance into heaven (Acts 2:38) and is the first plank in the Christian foundation (Hebrews 6:1). We do not help people to become true disciples of the Lord Jesus Christ unless we explain to them clearly that they cannot come to God until they are prepared to wholly agree with God on what He says about them.

It may help us to see better what repentance is by looking for a moment *at what it is not*. Repentance is not being sorry for the consequences of our sin, neither is it remorse at being found out. The difference can be seen clearly from the experiences described for us in the New Testament of Judas Iscariot and Simon Peter. Both failed Christ in the hours prior to His crucifixion, but we read that "Peter went out and wept bitterly", while "Judas went out and hanged himself". Peter's actions led him to repentance, while Judas' led him to suicide. One was filled with repentance – the other was filled with remorse.

Repentance is necessary for an entrance into heaven.

O God, when I see so much hanging on a word, enable me to know in the depths of my being the reality of a truly repentant heart. In Jesus' Name. Amen.

WHAT SIN REALLY IS
For Reading and Meditation: James 4:7–10

"As you come close to God you should be deeply sorry, you should be grieved, you should even be in tears." (v. 9, J. B. Phillips)

We are laying down the firm principle that repentance is the first step in discipleship. It means more than being sorry for the trouble we have caused, and involves a turning from self-centredness in which we accept that we are wrong and God is right. Man's real sinfulness consists in his refusal to honour God as God. It is not just a denial of the existence of God, nor even a rejection of the philosophical concept of God. We can believe in God, attempt to worship Him, and still run our lives on our own terms. Sin is more than wrong-doing, for it consists in allowing self to be firmly fixed in the centre of our beings, which really is the part which God made for Himself. Crime is breaking the laws of the state, but anarchy challenges the very right of the state to rule. *Sin is anarchy* in which we challenge God's right to rule from within the centre of our beings. Sin rules, in other words, by keeping self at the centre of our personalities rather than God; and so salvation from sin is also salvation for ourselves.

TOPPLING SELF FROM THE THRONE

So deeply ingrained is our basic self-centredness that there is no way, apart from repentance, by which self can be toppled from the throne. When we become thoroughly ashamed of ourselves for pushing God out of the centre of our lives – the part He made to be reserved for Himself – then we are closing in on the kind of repentance about which the New Testament is so clear. "Come close to God and he will come close to you. Realise that you have sinned and get your hands clean again" (v. 8, J. B. Phillips).

Man's real sinfulness consists in his refusal to honour God as God.

Lord Jesus, I see so clearly that my greatest sin is to keep You out of that part of me which You made for Yourself – my spirit. I give You that and everything else I have today. I pull down the flag and surrender. You are truly my Lord. Amen.

WE MUST *BEGIN* RIGHT

For Reading and Meditation: Matthew 16:21–28

"Then Jesus said to his disciples, 'If anyone would come after me, he must deny himself and take up his cross and follow me.' " (v. 24)

The deeper we go into this subject of discipleship the more we can see that no school was ever so strictly guarded, and yet there is none so easy of access. No bar of race, colour, caste or age stands across the entrance – *all* may come providing they submit to the entrance conditions.

COMPLETE SELF-SURRENDER

This raises the point: Why does Christ insist on such complete and utter self-surrender right at the outset? Would it not be better if He approached us more gently, then having got us in, tempered His challenge to our rate of progress? The answer is simple. If He is to keep us free from evil, then He must have the whole territory of our lives fully surrendered into His hands. Temptation seeks to find a foothold in our lives on which it can fasten, then, once this is accomplished, it goes on to establish a bridgehead over which it sends its sappers to fortify the position and take over control.

TOO EASY

Christ makes it clear *from the beginning* that He cannot consent to be excluded from territory which the enemy could use to undermine His authority and weaken His control. Many of the troubles which some Christians have stem simply from the fact that they came into the kingdom of God too easily. They never learned how important it is, in those early stages, to deal a death blow to self-centredness, and so they limp along in the Christian life, with no real understanding of what it is all about. The stern words of Christ, which He utters to all those about to submit to Him, are not said to frighten us, but to fortify us.

The stern words of Christ are not said to frighten us but to fortify us.

I am grateful to You, dear Lord, for holding me to this simple and clear plan of salvation. If I cannot submit at the beginning of my life with You, then how will I be able to submit at a later stage? Thank You for showing me this. In Christ's Name. Amen.

UNLESS!

For Reading and Meditation: John 3:1–8

"… 'no-one can see the kingdom of God unless he is born again.' " (v. 3)

We continue to look at the importance of conversion as a prelude to Christian discipleship. In speaking of the new birth and conversion, Jesus used a very decisive word in both cases – *Unless.* Is this "Unless" of Jesus too harsh and too narrow? I believe not.

THE POWER OF CONVERSION

Many have tried to reproduce the character of Christ in their lives by religious striving, but to no avail. The best that religion can produce (apart from conversion) is just not good enough to pass the test of life. St. Theresa, for example, tells how for many years she coldly and mechanically went about her tasks, fulfilling her round of duties, and saying her prayers. Then one day she entered the chapel, as she had done on many a previous occasion, but this day things turned out differently. As her eyes fell upon the cross she saw it in a new light, and for the first time understood the love of God as manifested in the suffering of His Son. She felt in a *personal* way, that that love was meant for her. Falling upon her knees she surrendered her whole being to the Lord Jesus Christ, and rose to begin a new and exciting life. Following this wonderful experience in the chapel, wherever she went and whenever she spoke, her words produced faith in the hearts of those who listened to her, and from that day her ministry took on a strange eternal power.

What had happened? A devoted and dedicated nun had experienced the power of a true conversion. Before this she had been working to be saved. Now she was working because she was saved. And between those two statements there is a world of difference.

The character of Christ cannot be reproduced by religious striving.

Father, You are overwhelming me with Your generous grace. I thought once that I had to climb up to heaven to bring You down. But You have come down to bring me up. I am saved not by works, but by grace. Thank You, Father. Amen.

NO SUBSTITUTE FOR CONVERSION

For Reading and Meditation: Psalm 19:1–11

"The law of the Lord is perfect, converting the soul: the testimony of the Lord is sure, making wise the simple." (v. 7, AV)

We must spend another day on making clear the supreme importance of conversion as a prelude to Christian discipleship.

A world-travelled preacher, whose ministry took him to over forty countries, said before he died, "Probably two-thirds of the membership of the churches in which I have preached, know little or nothing about conversion as a personal and experiential fact." His conclusion was drawn from experiences within one particular type of denomination, of course, but if I was asked to speculate on the number of people in churches of all denominations who lack a definite personal encounter with the Living Christ I would say it would number about one-third.

MINISTERS AND PROFESSORS OF THEOLOGY

In some denominations – not all – there are ministers who have never known what it is to be "born again" and lack a definite personal experience with the Lord Jesus Christ. How can a congregation be brought to a saving knowledge of Jesus Christ if the minister lacks a personal faith? A senior professor in a theological cemetery (oops! I meant seminary) said, "The term 'born again' is not a term we use in this seminary." A student who passed out of that same seminary with a theological degree remarked to a friend, "What do people mean when they talk about self-surrender? I never heard that term in seminary."

A few decades ago an archbishop's report on evangelism said, "The Church is more a field, rather than a force for evangelism." Things haven't changed much. There are still far too many in our churches who lack a dynamic personal encounter with the Lord Jesus Christ.

Far too many in our churches lack a dynamic personal encounter with the Lord Jesus Christ.

O God, when so many are stumbling in darkness, trying to work for their salvation, I am so grateful that You have shown me the true way. Receive my humble thanks – in Jesus' Name. Amen.

OUT OF STEP

For Reading and Meditation: Luke 9:18–26

" 'But what about you?' he asked. 'Who do you say I am?' Peter answered, 'The Christ of God.' " (v. 20)

The importance of accepting the Lordship of Christ right at the beginning of our Christian experience is nowhere more evident than in this chapter before us right now. The question, "Who do you say I am?" brought forth from Simon Peter the confession of Christ's Lordship, "You are the Christ, the Son of the living God" (Matthew 16:16). In this incident there can be no doubt that Jesus was trying to bring home to His disciples the truth that lay at the heart of His redemptive mission, and His being the Son of God, namely His willingness to give Himself. "The Son of Man must suffer many things ... and be killed" (v. 22). In a direct challenge to them *all* Jesus then said, "If anyone would come after me, he must deny himself and take up his cross daily and follow me" (v. 23).

His intention was to show them that just as the cross of self-surrender lay at the heart of His being the Son of God, so the cross of self-surrender lay at the heart of their discipleship. The Bible says they did not understand this saying, and they were afraid to ask Him about it (v. 45). They were afraid to ask because it might involve them in a deeper challenge than they were willing to face.

The cross of self-surrender lay at the heart of their discipleship.

FAILURE TO UNDERSTAND

The failure to understand His statement, and all that it involved for them, began to show in their relationships: (1) "An argument started among the disciples as to which of them would be the greatest" (v. 46); (2) "Lord, do you want us to call fire down from heaven to destroy them?" (v. 54); (3) "Master, we saw a man driving out demons in your name and we tried to stop him" (v. 49).

Lord, how true it is that when I am out of step with You, I am out of step with everyone else. Help me to see that when I give You Your rightful place, all of life will drop into the right perspective. Amen.

A SAD COMMENTARY

For Reading and Meditation: Luke 9:51–62

"When ... James and John saw this, they asked, 'Lord, do you want us to call fire down from heaven to destroy them?' " (v. 54)

We saw yesterday how the disciples' refusal and fear to face up to the challenge of Christ's Lordship began to show up in their relationships with Christ and each other.

It always does. From the moment the disciples made the marvellous discovery that Jesus was the Son of God, not a single thing was done right by them, or others who figure in this chapter. Could it be that they committed themselves to the fact of His Lordship in an intellectual sense only, while their emotions continued to be held in the grip of an unsurrendered self? In the moment of revelation when they discovered that Jesus Christ was the Son of God, you would have thought that the disciples would have looked at Him and each other in a new light, and with different attitudes. Instead they tripped over themselves in every single happening and relationship. The basis of their failure, so it seems to me, was the fact that their acceptance of Christ's Lordship was *intellectual* and not *emotional*. With their minds they accepted His Lordship, but their emotions had not been affected, and continued to manifest a desire to have their own way.

SELF-INTEREST DOMINATES

Not only did the disciples fail to grasp the point, but other would-be disciples missed it also: "He said to another man, 'Follow me.' But the man replied, 'Lord, first let me go and bury my father' " (v. 59). "Still another said, 'I will follow you, Lord; but first let me go back and say good-bye to my family' " (v. 61). These men made it clear that their own self-interest dominated their thoughts, and is a sad commentary on what happens to our relationships when we belong to ourselves and not to Him.

Did their emotions continue to be held in the grip of an unsurrendered self?

O God, I fling myself at Your feet to be touched in every part of my being. Strengthen me to know Your Lordship, not only in my intellect, but in the area of my emotions too. Then I know that Your way will be my way. Amen.

HE MUST BE FIRST

For Reading and Meditation: Luke 9:57–62

"Jesus replied, 'No-one who puts his hand to the plough and looks back is fit for service in the kingdom of God.' " (v. 62)

We must spend one more day on looking at this important chapter, which spells out for us the difficulties that befall us when we accept with our minds the Lordship of Christ, but fail to let that decision affect our hearts. The words of our text today sum up the sadness of our Lord Jesus Christ as He faced a would-be disciple with the reality of his own heart. *"No-one who puts his hand to the plough and looks back is fit for service in the kingdom of God."*

NO GOING BACK

These three men in this section of the chapter came very near to being great men. They were would-be disciples, and for a moment they are caught in the glare of a spiritual *tête à tête* with Christ, only to fade into oblivion as they make clear by their actions that their commitment was simply marginal and not central. The very first condition of being one of Christ's disciples is a willingness and readiness to *put Him first* – beyond thought, feeling and personal desire. Those who take up the plough and look back are indicating by that look a spirit of self-centredness in which they say, "I wonder whether or not I did the right thing." They are like the person of whom it was said, "He cared little for his character, but everything for his reputation."

When we try to surrender our reputations and leave our characters untouched, then we fail to pass the first test of *discipleship*. There are many in the Church of Jesus Christ who are marginally surrendered but self sticks out in all they do. Success in *discipleship* depends on who is first – you, or Christ.

Put Christ first – beyond thought, feeling and personal desire.

O God, I don't want to keep shirking, dodging, and bypassing the challenges of Your Spirit to my heart. I will surrender to You in the central parts of my being, and then I know that what happens on the margin will be under Your control. Amen.

COUNTING THE COST

For Reading and Meditation: Luke 14:28–32

" 'Suppose one of you wants to build a tower. Will he not first sit down and estimate the cost ...?' " (v. 28)

Even the most casual reader of the New Testament cannot help but notice that, whenever Jesus Christ had a crowd before Him, He would usually start talking to them about some aspect of discipleship.

A DESCRIPTION OF HIMSELF

Men were often drawn to Jesus because of the demonstration of His miracles, but He rarely let those occasions pass without uttering some serious and sobering challenge to their personal lives. It was on such an occasion that Christ presented this famous story about a man who, wanting to build a tower, first sat down to count the cost. Some have interpreted this story to mean that each person should sit down and consider the cost involved in becoming a disciple. This is one interpretation, of course, but I think the real one is best brought out by the great expositor G. Campbell Morgan, who claims that Christ was using these illustrations of a man about to build a tower, and a king about to go to war, as a description of Himself. Christ had come to this world to establish a kingdom and wage a spiritual warfare of tremendous proportions. He was justified, therefore, in first evaluating the cost and outlining clearly to people the standard He needed them to reach if they were to assist Him in building His kingdom. Christ, then, says G. Campbell Morgan, is the *builder* who is in this world to build a kingdom for His Father. He has a job to do and a battle to win – hence, right from the start, He spells out in no uncertain terms the demands of discipleship. He has need of men and women who will not easily give up. Will you be one?

> *Jesus Christ has need of men and women who will not easily give up.*

O God, now I see why the demands of discipleship are so rigorous. You are looking for spiritual stalwarts to work with You in building Your kingdom. Lord, help me to be one. In Christ's Name. Amen.

UPSET – TO BE SET UP

For Reading and Meditation: Matthew 10:34–39

" 'Don't imagine that I came to bring peace to the earth! No, rather, a sword.' " (v. 34, TLB)

We are discovering that Christian discipleship is different from every other form of discipleship in the world today, for it demands a radical obedience.

Christ sets the agenda and draws up the rules. He prepares the contract and records all the stipulations. Christian discipleship is not a business relationship between two equals – it is a relationship between a Master and His disciple. Christ is the Lord – we are His subjects.

I struggled against this as a teenager, for I was willing at one time to surrender to God's will if He would show me what He wanted me to do. Then I realised that I was trying to spell out conditions to God before I trusted Him – rather like asking God to fill in a cheque for me, and then I would gladly sign it. Finally I surrendered to God without any conditions, and that day I really met Him in a way I have never forgotten.

STUBBORN RESISTANCE

With most people the first approach of God to their hearts is met with a strong and stubborn resistance. This is because there is an instinctive reaction in all of us against a seeming intruder who attempts to take over our lives. The instinct of self-preservation rises up to oppose an outside invader and establishes barriers of different kinds. When Jesus first appeared on this earth we are told that "King Herod ... was disturbed, and all Jerusalem with him" (Matthew 2:3). Jesus sparked off trouble as soon as He appeared in the world, and no wonder, for His coming always demands a change. His upsets, however, are always designed to set us up.

Christian discipleship is a relationship between a Master and His disciple.

O God, how true it is that Your coming spells trouble to those parts of my being that want to remain unchanged. Help me in these days of challenge not to draw back, but to submit to all You are seeking to do in my life. In Christ's Name. Amen.

DISCIPLESHIP AND DISCIPLINE

For Reading and Meditation: 1 Corinthians 9:19–27

"... everyone who competes for the prize is temperate (disciplined) in all things ..." (v. 25, NKJ)

Having firmly fixed in our minds the meaning and importance of discipleship, and having understood the need for Christ to be the central force and fact of our lives, we ask ourselves – *what next?*

The answer can be summed up in one word – *discipline*. In some ways the word sounds grim and foreboding, but let us not be put off by this, for the word has important aspects which are going to help us become effective disciples. Paul realised that to be an effective disciple of the Lord Jesus Christ required discipline in all areas of his being. Forces that are unharnessed roam everywhere and get nowhere – except into trouble. When our mental, physical and spiritual energy is harnessed to God's ends then the discipline provides a drive that nothing can gainsay.

THE SURGEON WHO LIMPED

Dr Charles Mayo, one of the world's greatest surgeons, suffered with lameness in one of his legs. When a friend gently questioned him about it, he said, "There is a passage in the Bible, which says, 'They made me the keeper of the vineyards; but mine own vineyard have I not kept.' I saw this coming on, but I would not pay heed."

Apparently he had not disciplined himself to heed the advice he had given to others, and so he dragged a lame leg through life as the result.

We must be disciplined, or remain decadent.

Many of us similarly limp along the highway of discipleship dragging a lame leg behind us, because we have never taken the trouble to discipline ourselves in some area of our lives. Spiritual shortsightedness and unconcern strike back at us in a decaying spiritual experience. We must be disciplined, or remain decadent.

Lord Jesus, help me to face the challenge of this word today, and enable me to see that Your discipline is but the doorway through which I pass into greater spiritual development. Amen.

WHAT IS REAL FREEDOM?
For Reading and Meditation: Galatians 5:1–13

*"It is to freedom that you have been called, my brothers.
Only be careful that freedom does not become mere
opportunity for your lower nature ..." (v. 13, J. B. Phillips).*

One of the evidences of being a true disciple of the Lord
Jesus Christ is a willingness to accept the necessary
disciplines which go toward the building of our personal
character.

LIBERTY AND LICENCE

In an undisciplined age, such as we live in at present, when
liberty and licence have replaced law and loyalty, we sorely
need to see the proper Scriptural relationship between discipline and discipleship. In some churches the message of
"free grace" has been presented in such a way that it has
weakened character.

   This is what had been happening in the Galatian churches,
causing the apostle to issue this stern rebuke, "Do not make
your freedom an opening for the flesh" (v. 13, Moffatt's
translation). Liberty had been turned into licence, and
now *discipline* was needed in order to restore their spiritual balance. The truth that Christ has set us free must be
balanced by the equally important truth that the Christian
life requires discipline, if the forces of our being are to move
in the right direction.

   A young Christian came up to me after a recent meeting
and said, "Now that I am a Christian I am free from the
demands of the Law, so I see nothing wrong in sleeping
with my girl friend before we are married." I pointed out to
him that while he was perfectly free to do what he liked,
he was not free to choose the consequences, and those
consequences would keep their score in his spirit, his soul
and his body. "Freedom," said someone, "is not the right to
do what we want, but the power to do what we ought."

> *"Freedom
> is not the
> right to do
> what we
> want, but
> the power
> to do what
> we ought."*

**Heavenly Father, quietly I am coming to the conclusion that I
am only truly free when I am circumscribed by Your control.
Help me to realise that I do not have to endure freedom – but
enjoy it. Amen.**

KEEPING TO THE TRACKS

For Reading and Meditation: John 8:28–36

" '... If you hold to my teaching, you are really my disciples. Then you will know the truth, and the truth will set you free.' " (vv. 31–32)

We are seeing that the way of discipleship is a way of discipline. We ended yesterday by saying that "Freedom is not the right to do what we want, but the power to do what we ought."

CHRIST'S JOY

Does that mean that if we can't do what we want, we become cynical and disagreeable people? It need not, for when we partake of Christ's joy, then our joy is complete – for His joy and ours are then the same. God does not impose His joy upon us in order to make us happy against our will, but in receiving His joy, our own joy discovers its true fulfilment. We must get hold of this truth until it becomes part and parcel of our whole being. There is an idea in some Christian circles that our will and God's will are totally alien, but the truth is our own will cannot function at its highest level until it finds *His*. Both God's will and my will are made for each other, and it is only when *I joyfully submit to His designs* that I realise my full potential as a person.

SHORT CUT

Imagine a train trying to save time by attempting to take a short cut across a field where there are no railway tracks. How far would it get? In its search for freedom, all it would experience is restriction, and curtailment of its liberty. A train is free to enjoy its potential when it runs along the tracks for which it was designed. Then, and only then, can it fulfil its real destiny. Our lives can only enjoy the freedom God has ordained for us when we stay on the tracks which His love has provided. When we keep to them we experience liberty; when we move off them we get bogged down in despair.

Our own will cannot function at its highest level until it finds God's will.

Father, when I run along the rails of Your true purposes for my life I am fulfilled, but when I move off them I am frustrated. Help me to stay on the tracks. In Christ's Name. Amen.

"Be Careful Little Eyes"
For Reading and Meditation: Matthew 18:1–11

" 'If your hand or your foot causes you to sin, cut it off ... And if your eye causes you to sin, gouge it out ...' " (vv. 8–9)

Jesus outlines for His disciples here the importance of being disciplined at the place of the *hand*, the *foot*, and the *eye*.

The hand

The hand is the part of us which takes hold of things – it is the part that grasps what we want. Never take hold of anything unless you want that thing to take hold of you. Some people grasp things, only to find that they have been gripped by the thing they grasped. *We need to be disciplined at the place of the hand.*

The foot

The foot is the part we use to approach things, and we should never make a move toward anything, unless we feel sure that we can safely grasp it without doing damage to our spiritual lives. Some people enjoy the excitement of walking toward things they know to be unspiritual and unchristian, solely for the pleasure they feel in being able to about-turn at the last moment. This is a dangerous way to live, and many who have indulged in this habit have been tragically ensnared. *We need to be disciplined at the place of the foot.*

The eye

The eye is the part of us which surveys things and then sends a message to our brain to propel us in that direction. We must be careful what we look upon – remember the Sunday School song, "Be careful little eyes what you see"? It's good up-to-date advice, *for we must be disciplined at the place of the eye.*

"I don't believe in running away from temptation," a young man once said to me. "I believe in staying to fight." Better if he had run away, for his record revealed a serious moral downfall. It's better to build a fence at the top of a hill, than to build a hospital at the bottom.

It's better to build a fence at the top of a hill, than a hospital at the bottom.

Lord Jesus, Your words, spoken so long ago, have a special application to my daily experience. Help me to know the disciplined life at the place of my hands, my feet, and my eyes. For Your Name's sake. Amen.

A VITAL DIFFERENCE

For Reading and Meditation: Psalm 34:1–11

"Fear the Lord, you his saints, for those who fear him lack nothing." (v. 9)

To understand God's purpose in disciplining His children, it is necessary to observe the difference between two things – fear and respect.

FEAR

The Bible uses the word "fear" in two ways: (1) as a form of anxiety, and (2) as a form of respect. As Christians, it is right and proper that we have a deep respect for the Almighty, but we must also see that God does not expect us to live out our days filled with anxiety, apprehension, and dread. Some parents attempt to influence their children through the use of fear and anxiety, but God does not deal with *His* children on this level.

I heard of one woman who, wanting to teach her child the rules of the road, took her down to a busy traffic intersection and shouted as each car approached, "Look out – here comes a car!" The child soon learned how to keep out of the way of approaching cars, but she also developed an unhealthy fear of all traffic conditions. One of the great goals of parenthood is to so train and discipline children that they develop respect without fear.

PUNISHMENT AND DISCIPLINE

This brings us to the question: Does God inflict punishment upon His children as a necessary part of Christian discipline? If we see the clear distinction which the Scripture gives between punishment and discipline, then the answer must be "No". God's punishment is the administering of just retribution for misdeeds, but discipline is the method He uses to correct wrong behaviour and develop our relationship as His sons. Christ took our *punishment* at the cross, so now that we are God's children, we are not under punishment, but under discipline. The difference is vital.

As Christians, we are not under God's punishment, but under God's discipline.

O God, how can I ever thank You enough for bearing my punishment at Calvary. Now all Your actions toward me are not retributive, but remedial, and are directed toward my personal growth. Thank You, Father. Amen.

DISCIPLINE'S DIVINE DESIGN
For Reading and Meditation: Romans 12:1–10

"I appeal to you therefore, brethren, by the mercies of God, to present your bodies as a living sacrifice ..." (v. 1, RSV)

We are considering the difference between punishment and discipline, and we are seeing that once we become Christians, the threat of punishment is forever removed. Our relationship with God following conversion is not as a *sinner,* but as a *son.*

Thereafter all God's actions toward us are aimed at producing spiritual maturity and growth.

CHALLENGE TO DEDICATION

The greatest challenge to dedication to be found anywhere in the New Testament is based not on the judgment of God, but on His mercy. "I appeal to you therefore, brethren, by the *mercies* of God, to present your bodies as a living sacrifice." God doesn't attempt to coerce His children by scaring them with the threat of punishment, neither does He pounce upon us when we do wrong so as to even the score. His disciplines follow a divine design and are carefully, lovingly, and tenderly worked out, to develop our maturity, and promote our spiritual growth.

FIVE STEPS

After searching for many years to see the design of God in disciplining His children, I have discovered in the Scripture the following steps: (1) At conversion the aspect of *punishment* ceases, for all judgment has been borne by the Son. (2) God's appeals to correct behaviour are based, not on His ability to punish, but on His ability to love. (3) In His Word He lays down clear guidelines as to how we should live. (4) He makes clear what will happen if we obey, and also what will happen if we disobey. (5) When we disobey He intervenes to correct us, not in anger, or with a desire to get even, but with the deepest and tenderest love. Isn't God a wonderful Parent?

Our relationship with God following conversion is not as a sinner, *but as a* son.

O God, what release this concept brings to my life. Your disciplines are not directed in anger, but with the deepest love. You hurt me only in order to bring me to my fullest maturity. You are indeed a wonderful Father. Amen.

DISCIPLINED TO BE LIKE JESUS
For Reading and Meditation: Luke 6:39–45

" 'A disciple is not above his teacher, but everyone who is perfectly trained will be like his teacher.' " (v. 40, NKJ)

We must be careful in our understanding of the disciplines which discipleship demands that we don't finish up living by rule of thumb. A person who simply follows rules, and knows little of a vital daily personal contact with the Lord in prayer, will end up being an uncreative person.

ARTESIAN OR ARTIFICIAL

At first, of course, the disciplines we impose on ourselves, such as meeting the Lord daily in a personal Quiet Time, will be hard and rigorous. Gradually, however, they will become a natural part of our lives, and will turn out to be *artesian*, rather than *artificial*.

The disciplines involved in learning to play the violin, for example, can be extremely demanding in the early days, but later, when the person becomes proficient, there seem to be no rules that can hold him. An expert violinist may appear to be obeying some creative urge within him, as he brings out of the strings the most delightful music, but it is the *disciplines* which produce the creativity and control. The laws have become a liberty. Don't just rely on the fact that the Scripture gives you guidelines on how to act in times of difficulty, but keep yourself spiritually fit so that when you are suddenly brought face to face with a problem, you know *instinctively* how to act. Remember that the purpose of Christian discipline is not to make *you*, but to make you like Christ. We must never forget that the ultimate goal of discipleship is to make us like Jesus. We are being discipled into Christlikeness.

Keep yourself spiritually fit so that you know instinctively how to act.

O God, when I see that the goal of all Your discipline is to make me like Jesus, then I joyfully submit to every pressure of Your hand. Your ends are my ends. Amen.

TESTS BECOME TESTIMONIES

For Reading and Meditation: John 7:14–18

" 'If anyone chooses to do God's will, he will find out whether my teaching comes from God ...' " (v. 17)

Although the word "disciple" means a learner, this does not mean that we sit like students in a classroom storing up facts and information about the Lord Jesus Christ. Each truth He unfolds has to be lived out in practical situations, where it can be fully understood. No sooner does Christ begin to reveal some new truth to one of His disciples than He opens up some special circumstance in which that truth can be tested.

If, for example, you have a need to understand more about forgiving others, then you can be sure that it will not be long before you find yourself in a situation where you will be called upon to do just that. If, on the other hand, God sees that you have a particular need of more patience, then He will engineer a set of circumstances in which that patience will be tested.

HANDS-ON EDUCATION

You see, all your affairs are in the hands of a Master-Teacher who knows the value of a "hands-on" education. Each disciple must be tested, point by point, before he can move on to other things, and God's examinations are designed for the personal benefit of each one of His pupils. There are no "memory exercises" in this school, for each lesson has to be lived out in terms of personal experience. No one can learn tomorrow's lessons until he has covered the groundwork that is needed for today, any more than a child can be taught geometry until he has first learned how to add and subtract. So apply yourself willingly to all that He wants to teach you today, and tomorrow will yield a whole new scale of values in the exciting world of Christian discipleship.

Apply yourself willingly to all that He wants to teach you today.

O God, what relief sweeps through me as I discover that all my tests are designed by You, and that You expect no more from me than I am capable of giving. Thank You, Father. Amen.

THE LAW OF LOVE

For Reading and Meditation: James 1:19–27

"But if anyone keeps looking steadily into God's law for free men, he will not only remember it but he will do what it says, and God will greatly bless him ..." (v. 25, TLB)

We are seeing that the Christian disciple is not committed to a principle, but to a Person – that Person being none other than the Lord Jesus Christ. Principles are extremely impersonal and cannot produce a Christlike character. But Christ meets us Person-to-person, and produces a response in us which no precept could possibly achieve.

LEGALISTS

Those who simply commit themselves to the rules they find in the Bible become *legalists*. Legalists laboriously follow the laws but have little joy. They are often intolerant of the joy of others, and fall into the trap which ensnared the Pharisees of long ago. Once we understand that our salvation does not depend on a slavish obedience to law we turn to a new freedom, only to find a new kind of bondage – one that is not restrictive, but releasing. It is the bondage of being in love. Christians who are set free from a life of slavish obedience to rules, and live under the inspiration of the law of love, serve God, not because they *have* to, but because they *want* to. Thousands of Christians go on day after day attempting to serve God under an encroaching legalism which stifles their spiritual growth, and paralyses their every effort.

In my teens I knew two people who approached the Christian life from opposite extremes. One said, "I will follow all the rules and become a Christian." The other said, "No rules for me. I am not saved by works anyway, so it doesn't matter how I live." Both were wrong because they were following concepts rather than Christ.

It is the bondage of being in love.

Blessed Lord Jesus, how glad I am that I am not tied to concepts, but related to You by a living faith. I am serving You not because I have to, but because I want to. Amen.

LOSSES BECOME GAINS

For Reading and Meditation: Galatians 6:1–10

"If he sows to please his own wrong desires, he will be planting seeds of evil and he will surely reap a harvest of spiritual decay and death ..." (v. 8, TLB)

We are looking together at the need for discipline in our Christian lives, and we come now to the subject of our *habits.* Many Christians continue to cling to habits such as smoking, drinking, sexual fantasies, evading responsibility, over-eating, and many other things, failing to see that these are an escape route down which they run whenever they feel the need for security.

HANDLING OUR HABITS

The question must be asked: *Is our security in Christ, or is it in things?* There is only one effective way of handling our habits, and that is to surrender them into the hands of the Lord Jesus Christ. If you try to fight them, you will only complicate the problem, but when you surrender them to Christ, He takes them, deals with them, and replaces the loss with spiritual gain.

When I first came into the Christian experience I tried hard to break the habit of smoking – but to no avail. I struggled and fought against the habit with all the energy I could muster – but nothing happened. An old Welsh miner who sensed my predicament said, "Don't fight it – surrender it." I thought at first that his advice was too simplistic, but I tried it, and it worked. Fighting the problem only made it loom larger in my mind and imagination, but when I surrendered the habit into Christ's hands a tremendous power flowed into my being – and I was free.

In overcoming habits, let us never forget that our basic egocentricity will raise its head and want to be included in bringing about a release. It is part of our carnal nature which looks for a reason to be proud.

Don't fight it – surrender it.

O God, save me from wanting to be my own deliverer, and show me that when I surrender to Your supreme power, I do not suffer a loss but achieve a gain. Thank You, Father. Amen.

STOCKING THE STORE

For Reading and Meditation: Matthew 12:34–37

"A good man from his good store produces good things, and a bad man from his bad store produces bad things." (v. 35, Weymouth)

Today we focus on the fact that habit can work with us, as well as against us.

During the first few years of my Christian experience, I was so utterly overwhelmed with the fact that God had saved me that I used to say "Praise the Lord" to everyone I met. An older Christian took me aside and suggested that I was getting into the habit of saying, "Praise the Lord," and that it lacked real meaning. I was extremely discouraged for a while, until I read a book by Billy Bray, in which he too was accused of saying "Praise the Lord" out of habit. He met such objections in his quaint way by saying, "It's a very good habit, and so few have it."

GOOD CHRISTIAN HABITS

It is possible to establish good Christian habits until you habitually take the Christian attitude in all situations. For example, try waking up each morning with this prayer on your lips, "Thank You, Lord, that nothing can happen today that You and I can't handle together." A wise old preacher used this prayer with great effect – and so can you. Every good habit dropped into the subconscious mind works there for good. Our text today tells us that "a good man from his good store produces good things". As good and evil come out of the storehouse of our minds, we should make it our aim to fill up the store with good things. Then, when we need to draw out a special supply to meet some emergency, we will find that what we have laid aside is readily accessible. Constantly fill your mind with thoughts of God's goodness, and you will find that good habits can work as effectively for you, as bad habits do against you.

Constantly fill your mind with thoughts of God's goodness.

Father, help me to daily lay aside in the storehouse of my mind those thoughts which will stand by me in moments of extreme testing. This I ask in Christ's Name. Amen.

THE TYRANNY OF THE URGENT
For Reading and Meditation: Ephesians 5:8–20

*"Live life, then, with a due sense of responsibility ...
Make the best use of your time, despite all the difficulties
of these days." (vv. 15–16, J. B. Phillips)*

Discipleship involves every Christian keeping a strict
discipline on his time.

What is time? Someone described it as that "brittle,
splintering thing which flies into fragments even as we think
of it". Nature is like a huge clockmaker's shop in which
thousands of timepieces are for ever ticking, and as Christ's
disciples, we are encouraged to make good use of our time.

THE RIGHT USE OF TIME

A simple principle to follow in relation to the right use of
time is this – if you haven't time for it, then it is either not
your task, or you need to re-establish your priorities. In
some instances we must discipline ourselves to refuse to take
on extra tasks – even though they may be good – for if we
respond to all the calls for help that come to us, we will
soon need help ourselves. In one country I visited, I saw a
sign that said, "Don't write – send a telegram". It would
have been more help to the people there if it had said,
"Don't telegram – write", for that would have encouraged
them to look ahead and anticipate situations, rather than
waiting to the last moment and feverishly telephoning or
sending a telegram. A person in this situation gets upset and
then upsets others. He demands that people atone for his
procrastination with an instant reply. One of the most
important things we need to do is to make sure that our
goals are God's goals. Sit down today, examine your life, and
ask yourself, "How much of what I am doing is really what
the Lord wants me to be doing?" Then cut out the things
that He shows you are irrelevant.

We need to make sure that our goals are God's goals.

**Lord, help me to be free from the tyranny of the urgent, and
instead enjoy life as You enjoyed it while You were here on
earth, so that I achieve more by doing less. Amen.**

CONTINUING IN HIS WORD

For Reading and Meditation: John 8:31–32

"... 'If you continue in my word, you are truly my disciples.' " (v. 31, RSV)

Disciples have this quality above all others – they delight in the words of their Master.

SPENDING TIME IN THE BIBLE

Show me a disciple and I will show you a person who spends a good deal of time in the Bible. He ponders it, prays over it, lives in it, works it out, and meditates in it as often as he is able. Some started well on the way of discipleship, but they have become spiritual casualties because they failed to "continue in the word". Discipleship means more than mustering an initial dedication to pass the entrance test – it involves a life of *continued obedience* to the demands and challenges of God's Word. First He reveals, then you obey. On and on it goes – He revealing, and you obeying until new vistas of Christian experience are opened up. But be sure of this – when you stop obeying, He stops revealing.

The story is told of the late F. B. Meyer and C. T. Studd, who shared a room speaking at a Christian convention. In the middle of the night, F. B. Meyer awoke to find C. T. Studd poring over an open Bible in the light of a small flickering candle.

"What are you doing, Charlie?" said F. B. Meyer.

The great man replied, "I have been going through the Gospels, looking at all the commandments of the Lord Jesus, and I have been placing a mark by the side of the ones I have not obeyed."

"And what is the result?" enquired F. B. Meyer.

C. T. Studd looked across the darkened room toward his friend, and with tears in his eyes said, "Oh, my heart is ashamed."

When you stop obeying, He stops revealing.

O God, I don't want to be a disciple who starts well but falls by the way, so help me, I pray, to face every challenge Your Word brings in the knowledge that You will always supply the power to meet it. Amen.

IS GOD A MAGICIAN?

For Reading and Meditation: Romans 5:1–11

"... knowing that trouble produces endurance, endurance produces character, and character produces hope – a hope which never disappoints us ..." (vv. 3–5, Moffatt)

A disciple must know how to discipline himself in relation to *courage*. Each time we refuse to face up to our problems, we deprive ourselves of a great deal of character.

COMFORTABLENESS

People without courage are what Nietzsche called "moral cows in their plump comfortableness". I heard of a husband who disliked his wife's brightly painted fingernails, and when he asked her to use something a little less gaudy, she said, "I couldn't face my friends if I did that – everyone else wears them like this." She ran the risk of losing her husband's affections because she lacked the courage to step out of line with the cocktail-circuit custom.

TROUBLE DEVELOPS CHARACTER

As Christ's disciples we must not faint at the approach of problems, for they have in them the possibility of developing our character and increasing our courage. Paul uses three steps in the passage before us today which help us to see the way in which trouble develops character. (1) Trouble leads to endurance; (2) endurance leads to character; and (3) character leads to hope. And this hope will never let us down, for it gives us the assurance that there are doors in every difficulty, and triumphs in every temptation.

The great Einstein is reported to have put a plaque over his desk which read, "God is a scientist – not a magician." Some people expect God to wave a magic wand each time they get into trouble, and make the trouble disappear. He can, but He won't, for He knows how to make the trouble serve *His* ends, and produce a sterling quality in the hearts of His disciples.

God knows how to make trouble serve His ends.

O God, can it be that I have been seeing You merely as a magician, rather than as a scientist? If so, then forgive me, for I am discovering that You are able, not just to remove troubles, but to use them for Your glory and my enrichment. Thank You, Father. Amen.

PERMISSIBLE INTOLERANCE
For Reading and Meditation: John 12:20–32

" '... unless a grain of wheat falls into the earth and dies, it remains alone; but if it dies, it bears much fruit.' " (v. 24, RSV)

It may seem strange to some to talk of intolerance in connection with the Christian Gospel, for the Scriptures teach us to show tolerance and restraint in almost all situations.

INTOLERANCE WITH ONESELF

There is one realm, however, where intolerance is permissible – and indeed encouraged – and that is in connection with oneself. James Denny said, "If God has really done something in Christ on which the salvation of the world depends, and if He has made it known, then it is a Christian duty to be intolerant of everything which ignores, denies, or explains it away." God most certainly has done "something in Christ" for the salvation of the world, and it is this concept that we must now bring to bear upon one of the most powerful hindrances to discipleship – namely, our inbred resistance toward the death of our self-centredness. All the energy of our flesh cries out against this, for the deep currents of our lives sweep forward toward the development and recognition of the self – yet to no good purpose.

NEW LIFE

The only way in which a disciple can let his Master's life break through his own is when he voluntarily submits to be crushed, broken, and pressed into the ground to die. Then, in due time, a new life will spring forth, which is not his, but the resurrection life of his Lord, to spread an influence abroad which no earthly power can gainsay. To die to self and rise again in His strength is to find the real meaning of Calvary, which gives way to a Resurrection, and a glorious Pentecost.

Die to self. Rise again in His strength.

Father, Your message is beginning to strike home and my nature shrinks from the challenge. Hold me fast in this strong current so that I will be swept toward Your perfect will, not away from it. In Christ's Name. Amen.

A LOVE THAT IS SUPREME

For Reading and Meditation: Luke 14:26

" 'If anyone comes to me and does not hate his father and mother, his wife and children ... he cannot be my disciple.' "

Enemies of the cross have fastened upon this verse as an illustration of the alleged extremism of the Gospel, but their objections are based on a false premise. The word "hate" is used here in a comparative sense with love for God, and the real meaning of this verse, as indeed some modern translations make clear, is this – "If any man prefer his father and mother he cannot be my disciple". The Amplified Bible states, "If any one ... does not hate his [own] father and mother ... *in the sense of indifference to or relative disregard for them in comparison with his attitude toward God ...* he cannot be My disciple."

A SEARCHING QUESTION

The Lord is certainly not suggesting that we should have animosity and enmity in our hearts toward our relatives, but rather that our love for Him should be so consuming that it makes every other love look like hatred in comparison. Perhaps we should pause for a moment to pick up this challenge and apply it directly to our hearts. Can we honestly say today that we love the Lord more than our parents, our husbands, our wives, our boyfriends, our girlfriends, or our children? It's a searching question, isn't it? Don't be discouraged if you find that you cannot answer this question with a positive "Yes", for, as we saw, the love we give to Him is but the reflection of the love He gives to us.

When you are willing to pull down all the barriers that prevent His love from flowing into you, then you will be able to love Him in return – with a love that allows no other rival to occupy the centre of your heart.

A love that allows no other rival to occupy the centre of your heart.

Lord, I am being challenged again today in a way from which my human nature shrinks. But pursue me, I pray, for deep in my heart I really long to be Yours. Help me, for unless You do, I am hopeless and helpless. In Jesus' Name. Amen

FORSAKING ALL
For Reading and Meditation: Luke 14:33

" 'In the same way, any of you who does not give up everything he has cannot be my disciple.' "

Many people spend a great deal of time explaining what this verse does not mean, but those who are eager to become true disciples of the Lord Jesus Christ embrace its challenge with joy.

What does it really mean to forsake all? It means a readiness and willingness to abandon all personal rights to reputation, possessions, fame, and ambitions, and to transfer the ownership of everything into the hands of the Lord Jesus Christ. In simple terms, it means that we give up our rights to all that is our own, and thereafter become a steward, rather than a proprietor.

We see this truth illustrated beautifully in the life of the great C. T. Studd. Having given away his entire fortune, soon after his conversion, he reserved about £3,400 for his new bride. Not to be outdone by her husband she gave away this remaining sum, and they started their married life together with nothing.

JIM ELLIOTT'S DIARY

The same kind of spirit dominated the life of Jim Elliott, who wrote in his diary, "Father, let me be weak, that I might lose my clutch on everything temporal. My life, my reputation, my possessions. Lord, let me lose the tension of the grasping hand. Even, Father, would I lose the love of *fondling*. Rather open my hand to receive the nail of Calvary, as Christ's was opened – that I, releasing all, might be released, unleashed from all that binds me now." Later he wrote some words which illustrate the point still further, "He is no fool who gives what he cannot keep, to gain what he cannot lose."

We give up our rights to all that is our own. We become a steward, rather than a proprietor.

Lord Jesus, how wonderfully true You are to life. You lay it bare before my eyes and show it as it really is. Help me to be just as open in my response to You this day. Amen.

A SERVANT'S HEART

For Reading and Meditation: John 13:1–17

" 'I tell you the truth, no servant is greater than his master ...' " (v. 16)

Christ's disciples must know what it means to have a servant's heart. In the beautiful passage before us today, we see a supreme example of how to serve each other in love.

Just prior to this incident the disciples had been caught up in a power struggle: "Also a dispute arose among them as to which of them was considered to be greatest" (Luke 22:24). From a human standpoint the situation looked hopeless. Christ, however, does not scold them, or even lecture them, but in wondrous love stoops down to serve them once again. The Scripture says, "Jesus, knowing that the Father had given all things into his hands, and that he had come from God and was going to God" (v. 3, RSV). There was no question in Christ's mind concerning His true identity – *He knew who He was!* From this position of security and dignity, He was free to put all His energies into the task of serving His disciples.

TRUE HUMILITY

We can only become servants in the true sense of the word when we have a clear understanding of who we are, and why we are here. This assurance gives us a stability and security from which we move out to others with perfect freedom, as all true humility flows out of a position of great strength. The disciples, with their competitive spirit, could never climb over the wall of their own egocentricity and pride to wash anyone's feet, so Christ demonstrates for them the essence of true humility, stooping to do for them what they were unwilling to do among themselves.

A supreme example of how to serve each other in love.

O God, give me a deep sense of my own uniqueness, so that from a position of security I can be free to channel all my energies into serving others. This I ask in Christ's Name. Amen.

For Reading and Meditation: 2 Corinthians 5:10–21

"He died for all so that all who live – having received eternal life from him – might live no longer for themselves, to please themselves, but to spend their lives pleasing Christ ..." (v. 15, TLB)

We are beginning to see that once we become Christ's disciples, we no longer belong to ourselves – but to Him.

The New Testament is quite clear about this. Once we belong to Christ we no longer live for ourselves, but for Him who gave Himself for us on the cross. Those who resist this truth will never understand the first principles of discipleship, for it raises a vital question right at the beginning of our Christian walk: *If we belong to Christ, can we honestly cling to something that is not a part of Him?* The challenge might sound severe and stern, but there is good reason for it. Christ has bought us with His own blood. We are His by sovereign right. To live as if we belonged to ourselves is to steal from Him that which is rightly His.

GIVING UP ALL FOR CHRIST

We have twice referred to C. T. Studd in these studies, but permit me a further reference which brings a great deal of clarification on this point. C. T. Studd answered the challenge in this way: "I had known about Jesus dying for me, but I never understood that if He died for me, then I didn't belong to myself. Redemption means 'buying back', so that if I belong to Him, either I had to be a thief and keep what wasn't mine, or else I had to give up everything to God. When I came to see that Jesus Christ had died for me, it didn't seem hard to give up all for Him."

If anyone is finding it difficult to give things up for Christ, then stop thinking about what you are giving up, and think of what He gave up for you. It is this thought – and this alone – which brings a full release.

Stop thinking about what you are giving up, and think about what He gave up for you.

Lord, let this word sink deep into every corner of my heart this day, until I am gripped more by the thought of what You gave up for me, than what I am giving up for You. Amen.

BAPTISM – AN IMPORTANT STEP

For Reading and Meditation: Matthew 28:16–20

" 'Therefore go and make disciples of all nations,
baptising them in the name of the Father and of the
Son and of the Holy Spirit.' " (v. 19)

N o serious study on the subject of Christian discipleship would be complete without some reference to the importance of water baptism.

VALID TODAY

Jesus commanded that those who become His disciples should be baptised "in the name of the Father and of the Son and of the Holy Spirit". This command of the Lord is as valid today as His command to preach the Gospel to all nations.

Once we have repented, and have confessed Jesus Christ as Lord, we should then be baptised by total immersion in obedience to this command. Baptism, among other things, enables you to make a public witness to the fact that you have entered into the experience of Christ's death, burial, and resurrection. The step of being immersed in water enables you to identify with the Lord Jesus Christ in His humiliation, and as you go into the water you are saying, in effect, "In the same way that Jesus Christ took my place in death, I now identify with Him so that I can share His death. Just as He died to settle the sin question, so I now submit to that same principle so that my old nature, with all its failings, may be buried with Him, and that I might rise again in the fullness of life which He demonstrated by His resurrection, and which I know is available to me by the same process."

What a wonderful moment it is when you emerge from the waters to bear witness to the fact that you share in Christ's victory over sin and death, and intend living in the power of His resurrection life – "dead to sin, and alive to God".

Being immersed in water enables you to identify with the Lord Jesus Christ.

Heavenly Father, if You are saying something to me about this matter that I have not been aware of before, then give me the courage and the wisdom to deal with it in the way that best glorifies You. In Jesus' Name I ask this. Amen.

KEEPING CHRIST CENTRAL

For Reading and Meditation: I Corinthians 11:23–34

"For whenever you eat this bread and drink this cup, you proclaim the Lord's death until he comes." (v. 26)

We are looking together at some of the commands which Christ issues to His disciples. Today we must study the importance of meeting with Him regularly before the Table of Communion. On the same evening in which Jesus washed the feet of His disciples, He also instituted a memorial of a New Covenant, and in the act of taking bread at the Passover Feast He indicated that the New Covenant was to be closely related to the event they were then celebrating, namely the deliverance of Israel from the slavery of Egypt.

ENRICHMENT

Each one of us needs to celebrate Holy Communion as often as possible for by so doing we participate in something that ministers to our spiritual growth and enrichment. *It enriches us practically*: in the act of taking bread and wine we remind ourselves of the need for Christ to be central to our existence. Pressures and problems tend to push Christ on to the margin of our experience, but the act of Communion pulls Him back into the centre where He belongs. *It enriches us evangelically*: it does this by forcefully reminding us that it is by blood we are cleansed, and there can be no other way of salvation than through the death and resurrection of our Lord Jesus Christ.

It enriches us prophetically: we are bidden to do this "until he comes". Our hearts therefore are reminded that one day He is going to return. *It enriches us devotionally*: through a simple meal of bread and wine we are brought into an attitude of deepest reverence, where physical things speak of spiritual realities, and through which we can more easily worship and adore.

> *Holy Communion ministers to our spiritual growth and enrichment.*

O God, I am amazed that on the eve of Your death You should give such time and attention to instituting something that would enrich my understanding of You in the years to come. All I can say is thank You, Lord Jesus. Thank You. Amen.

DISCIPLING

For Reading and Meditation: Matthew 28:16–20

*" 'Therefore go and make disciples of all nations ...
teaching them to obey everything I have
commanded you ...' " (vv. 19–20)*

We must spend at least one day on the subject which not so long ago caused a fair amount of controversy in the Church in Britain, namely that of *discipling*.

This is the concept of one person being discipled by another, for development and spiritual growth. The Greek word "to disciple" appears four times in the New Testament, and the key verse is of course the one before us now – our Lord's parting command to His apostles.

IS IT SCRIPTURAL?

The question we must ask ourselves is this: Is it Scripturally correct to link one person to another in a master-disciple relationship? I do not think so. While a great deal of benefit can come from an older and experienced Christian working with a younger and more immature Christian, we must be careful lest we lose sight of the blazing truth which shines everywhere in the New Testament, that we are to be *Christ's disciples*, and not disciples of each other. If it is argued that the ultimate aim of the human master-disciple relationship is to bring the disciple to a place of maturity where he can relate to Christ in a more meaningful way, then I believe the same end can be achieved through a properly constituted local church government in which each person, linked organically with the body, has the privilege of individual growth apart from the domination of one particular person – however good and spiritual he may be. To dominate a person is, in a human sense, demeaning, and in the new humanity it is even more questionable.

*We are to be **Christ's disciples**, and not disciples of each other.*

Heavenly Father, I am thankful for those You have appointed to help me mature in my Christian experience, but help me always to keep my eyes fully focused on You. In Christ's Name. Amen.

SUBMISSION

For Reading and Meditation: Hebrews 13:7–21

"Obey your leaders and submit to their authority. They keep watch over you as men who must give an account ..." (v. 17)

"**A**re you in submission to anyone?" This is a question increasingly being asked in Christian circles – and it demands a proper reply.

BODY-MINISTRY

Each one of us needs to be in submission to some spiritual authority, for to do so helps us to live Christian lives free from strain and anxiety. In a worldly culture that has lost its bearings on the subject of authority, it is encouraging to know that committed Christians are concerned about such matters. The truth is that, at this moment, the Church of Jesus Christ is beginning to see in a new way the importance of its body-ministry, and many Christians are sincerely concerned to discover more about how a believing community should operate as a living organism.

The New Testament requires all Christians to submit to each other (Ephesians 5:21) and goes on to catalogue submission in specific instances, such as wives to husbands, children to parents, servants to masters, younger to older, all Christians to secular government, and to those who rule over them in the Church. The Scripture teaches that those who rule must not impose or enforce their authority in the way authority is often enforced in the world, and invites Christians to voluntarily submit themselves to their leaders so that the Church can grow and develop as a healthy body.

The principle of submission is taught everywhere in the New Testament, and no one with a servant's heart will resist this, for submission brings about deep changes in our being which, in turn, produce a greater conformity to the Lord Jesus Christ.

Each one of us needs to be in submission to some spiritual authority.

O Father, I see clearly it is only when I am submitted to authority that I can wield authority. Unless I learn how to obey, I will never learn how to rule. Help me to understand this. In Christ's Name. Amen.

THE ESSENTIAL DYNAMIC
For Reading and Meditation: Acts 2:1–11

"All of them were filled with the Holy Spirit and began to speak in other tongues as the Spirit enabled them." (v. 4)

When Jesus Christ walked this world in company with His disciples, His personal presence became to them a tower of spiritual strength. He shared with them the principles of effective living, and taught them the important aspects of His heavenly kingdom.

THEY STRUGGLED FOR PROMINENCE
In some ways it seems strange that after three and a half years of training, the disciples still manifested a great degree of self-centredness, spitefulness, and animosity. Only a few days away from His death on the cross, they struggled for prominence, disputed among themselves as to who was the greatest, resented those who would not receive them in a Samaritan village, and asked that fire would be sent down from heaven! Despite their personal training at the hands of the Master, they were still obviously unfit to go and make disciples of others.

One of the reasons for this, I believe, was the fact that prior to His death on the cross, and His subsequent resurrection, Christ was just *with* them, and not *in* them. He shared with them the principles that governed His own life, but, having received all the facts, something more was needed – the facts needed to be set on fire! Principles by themselves are inadequate to turn a group of self-centred men into an army of blazing disciples. They needed something more than Christ *with* them – they needed Christ *in* them. In the Upper Room, this is exactly what took place. The same Christ who had walked with them, now moved inside them to give them the dynamic they needed. Not only were they in Him, but He was in them – and this made all the difference.

Christ was just with them, and not in them.

Heavenly Father, if the disciples who walked with You needed the ministry of the Spirit to set them on fire, then so do I. Let the flame of Pentecost descend on me today. Amen.

THE SECRET OF SUCCESS

For Reading and Meditation: Acts 2:12–21

"Then Peter stood up with the Eleven, raised his voice and addressed the crowd ..." (v. 14)

We consider today the fact that something dynamic must have happened to the disciples to turn them from the frightened men they were, into people who were completely invincible. Yesterday we came to the conclusion that it was because Christ had moved within them, by the power of the Holy Spirit, to share with them His risen life and power.

THE RESURRECTION OF CHRIST

He who had been *with* them, was now *in* them. The resurrection of Christ brought Him from the local to the universal, as prior to His death and rising again Christ's ministry had been very much limited to the geographical area of Palestine. Bursting through the bars of death, however, He entered a new dimension and, at Pentecost, shared with His disciples not just His principles, but His power.

PENTECOST

The disciples had gone as far as they could prior to Pentecost, and despite the fact that they had personally enjoyed Christ's presence for three and a half years, something more revolutionary was needed if they were to become His true followers. At Pentecost it happened. The risen Christ imparted to them the secret of His own success – the Holy Spirit – so that now they were not just slaves to a principle, but men who were submitted to His Person. He lived in them, moved in them, worked, thought, and ministered through them. Had there been no resurrection, it is doubtful whether we would have heard of those disciples again. They had received good training, and understood some fine spiritual principles, but Christ's discipleship is of a higher calibre – it needed His life to be lived out in them.

The secret of His own success – the Holy Spirit.

O God, the truth that I am not just a slave to a principle but vitally connected to a Person is growing in me. One of these days I am going to explode. Hallelujah!

MASTERED ON THE INSIDE

For Reading and Meditation: Acts 2:41–47

"Every day they continued to meet together ... They broke bread in their homes and ate together with glad and sincere hearts." (v. 46)

We must spend one more day looking at the reason for the remarkable difference in the disciples after they had received the Spirit at Pentecost.

AFTER PENTECOST

Prior to this experience, and during their period of training with the Lord Jesus Christ, the commands of the Master came to them from the outside. After Pentecost, however, when Christ in the power of the Holy Spirit moved inside their personalities, the commands were given from the inside. *It was this that made all the difference.* Before, they had been mastered from without – now they were mastered from within. Each one of us needs to be mastered at the central part of our beings. The co-ordinating centre needs to be taken over by the Lord Jesus Christ, and we must know an experience of discipleship which controls us, not only from the outside, but from the inside also.

HUNGRY FOR GOD

When we open ourselves to the flow of the Spirit within us, then the more of Him we receive the more of Christ we receive, for He comes in to make us whole. The Spirit is pretty powerful and pretty wonderful, but we must let Him *flow* into our beings. I am not concerned whether you identify it as the baptism, filling, charismatic experience – terms are important for doctrinal examination, but the simple fact of the matter is this – *are you hungry for God?* Do you long to know Him in all His fullness? Are you tired of a Christian experience that is lifeless and empty and vague and dry? Then open your being to the flow. Let Him fill you today.

Before, they had been mastered from without – now they were mastered from within.

O Father, open the windows of heaven and flood my life today with a deluge of Your Spirit such as I have never known before. Then help me to channel that power into a lifeline that will bring others to You. In Christ's Name. Amen.

A SOBERING THOUGHT

For Reading and Meditation: I Peter 3:8–17

"Who is going to harm you if you are eager to do good? But even if you should suffer for what is right, you are blessed ..." (vv. 13–14)

As we draw toward the end of our study on Christian discipleship, one remaining thought needs to be considered – the matter of *persecution*.

In our passage for today, the apostle Peter warns us about the pressure we can expect from society, and he encourages us at such times to revere Christ in our hearts. A true Christian witness will eventually produce persecution. It is interesting to note that the word "martyr" comes from the Greek word "martus", which also means "witness". We must face the fact that as the world gets darker, and the Church gets brighter, the contrast between the two will become so great that men will attempt to put out the light, as it inevitably adds to their sense of sin. Because of this, some of Christ's disciples may be called upon to be modern-day martyrs, and to sacrifice their lives in the cause of the Lord Jesus Christ. The day is not too far distant when the tide will turn against the Church, and true Christians will be persecuted for their faith. The reason why the Church continues to peacefully co-exist with modern-day society is because there is not enough vitality in the Church to produce a sufficiently striking contrast with the world.

NO SACRIFICE TOO GREAT

However, things are going to change; a wind is blowing in the Church which indicates that soon she will emerge "terrible as an army with banners" (Song of Solomon 6:10, RSV). At that time men will have no excuse for their sin, and will react with hostility toward a revived Church. The result, in some countries, may well be martyrdom. Let C. T. Studd have the last word: "If Jesus Christ be God, and died for me, then no sacrifice can be too great for me to make for Him."

A true Christian witness will eventually produce persecution.

O God, You have brought me face to face with a serious and sobering fact, but one that I need to recognise and appreciate. Help me to be faithful, no matter what happens. In Christ's Name. Amen.

EVERY CHRISTIAN A DISCIPLE

For Reading and Meditation: John 8:31–36

"... 'If you hold to my teaching,
you are really my disciples.' " (v. 31)

On this our last day of sharing together on the subject
of discipleship, let's cast our minds back and pinpoint
some of the things we have learned.

LEARNER

A disciple, we saw, is "a learner", or "a trained one", who
lives close to his Master, evaluates His words, and copies His
lifestyle. We come into the realm of discipleship through a
decision in which we surrender our egocentricity to Christ,
and admit Him into our lives as Lord. This initial surrender
and the act of repentance produces a clear conversion,
which sets the sails for an ongoing relationship with the
Lord Jesus Christ, in which He is seen as wholly right and
never wrong.

LIKE CHRIST

Discipleship, however, is not a slavish obedience to a set of
principles, but a living, vital contact with the Person of
Christ, who comes to indwell His disciples and live out His
dynamic life through them. Every Christian is expected to
be a first-class disciple, for there are no second-class citizens
in the kingdom of God. The goal of discipleship is not
simply to make *us,* but to make us like Christ. "For from the
very beginning God decided [that we] ... should become
like His Son" (Romans 8:29, TLB).

At Pentecost the Holy Spirit came to make Christ available to each one of us, and places Him, not at our sides to
be our instructor, but right at the core of our beings to be
the driving force of our personalities. A disciple is not
simply someone whom Christ teaches, but someone in
whom Christ *lives.*

A disciple
is someone
in whom
Christ
lives.

**O Lord Jesus, when the world stands in need of seeing what a
disciple of Christ is really like, I offer myself to You today in an
act of complete dedication. Come and live Your life in me, so
that the world will see that I am one of Your disciples. Amen.**